Colin,

Enjoy!

David W Port

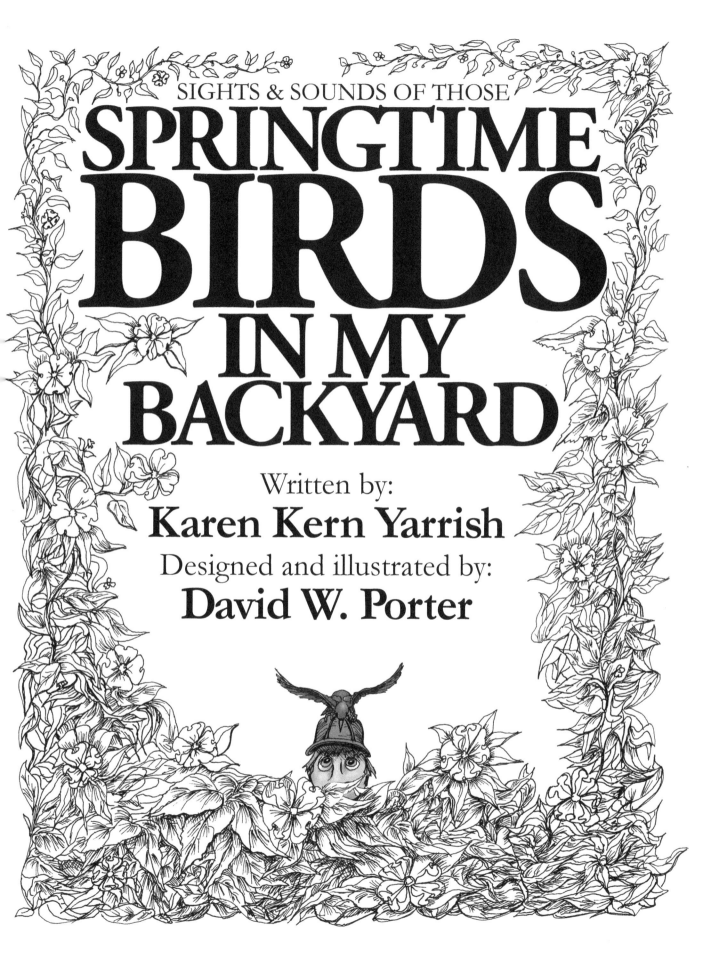

SIGHTS & SOUNDS OF THOSE

SPRINGTIME BIRDS IN MY BACKYARD

Written by:

Karen Kern Yarrish

Designed and illustrated by:

David W. Porter

Swingin' Bridge Books is an imprint of Keystone College.

Keystone College
One College Green
La Plume, PA 18440

www.keystone.edu

First Edition

Set in Garamond

Library of Congress Control Number: 2017959708

ISBN (Hardback Edition): 978-1-64042-700-6
ISBN (Paperback Edition): 978-1-64042-701-3

The author of this book, Karen Kern Yarrish, wishes to dedicate
the words in this book to her husband Craig for his unconditional love and support.

The designer and illustrator of this book, David W. Porter, wishes to dedicate the
artwork in this book to his wife Donna, son Jacob, and daughter Kaitlin.

It's a beautiful day to play,
In the early part of May,

But instead of playing with toys,
Jennifer stops and listens to a beautiful noise.

What she hears
isn't loud, crackling, or pinging,
No, this sound is soothing,
It is like singing!
What she has heard is not a simple word,
But the sweetest song-sound
of a small, tiny bird.
Looking up high in the old maple tree,
She spies
The cutest bird
She ever did see.
"Mama,
What kind of bird is that I see?"
Mama says,
"Why that is a...

...BLACK-CAPPED CHICKADEE.

He says his name,
Chick-a-dee-dee-dee,
and his family joins in with,
Fee-bee, fee-bee."

"Mama,
I hear another song,
Sounding like a whooo-whooo-whooo."
Then turning her head and looking above,
She spots the singer, It is a...

...MOURNING DOVE.

"Mama, now there's a black bird
With red on his wings."
"Yes, sweetie, and listen to him as he sings."
Oink-a-ree
Is the silliest sound
That they have yet heard.
The screeching, strong, song-sound,
Of the...

...RED-WINGED BLACK BIRD.

Jennifer's brother joins them
As they lie down on the grass,
"What are you two doing
looking up at the sky?" he asks.
Jennifer answers,
We are finding birds by looking up at the sky,
Listening as they sing songs, and
Watching them fly by."
Brother asks, "Who is the red bird,
With a crown for a topping?"
Mama answers,
"That's the mighty...

...CARDINAL.

He is singing,
What-a-cheer, what-a-cheer
Without stopping."

"Mama,
I did not know
That so many
birds live here."
"Oh yes,
And there are many more
ever so near.
Listen to that bird
With so much to say.
He is the
Boisterous but beautiful, bright...

...BLUE JAY.
He warns the other birds
When danger is around,
By making his loud
Jay-jay-jay sound."

"Look at that silly bird,
scampering down the tree head first."
"He's the...

WHITE-BREASTED NUTHATCH,

Calling yank-yank-yank

In full burst."

And on the grass a bird pulls at a worm. It is his favorite snack. He likes when they squirm. That bird is a...

...ROBIN.

He sings a happy song
As he sits on up.
The song goes like this,
Cheery-up, cheer-up.

"Look at that gray bird
With a tuft upon his head."
"That is the...

... TUFTED TITMOUSE,"

her mother said.
"He sounds like he is saying
Your brother's name, Peter."
Peter-Peter-Peter,
Sings the bird
from the
feeder.

"How about
The beautiful
Yellow and black bird
Over there?"
"That is the...

...AMERICAN GOLDFINCH,

Flying around without a care.
His song sounds like
Potato-chip, potato-chip-chip,
And he likes to eat
thistle seeds
Held fast with a grip."

"How about
the little bird
darting in and out?"
"That is a...

...RUBY-THROATED HUMMINGBIRD,

And he has lots of clout,
Because he is the only bird
That can fly forward and
Backward and hover as well.
He drinks nectar from flowers and
Feeders with a flowery smell.
If the throat is red, then it is a male,
If there is no red on the throat,
Then it is a female."

"Mama,"
Peter asks, "How can you tell
The boy and girl birds apart?"

Mama replies,
"The boys are more colorful;
Mother Nature is smart.
She designed it so the girls' feathers
Would blend in with the tree,
To keep her and her babies
safe from danger
So they won't be seen."

The Cardinal, American Goldfinch,
Ruby-Throated Hummingbird, and
Red-winged Blackbird males
Look very different
From the same bird females.

With the Black-Capped Chickadee, Blue Jay
Robin, Mourning Dove,
and White-Breasted Nuthatch,
It is harder to tell,
They look quite similar,
With the same
colored feathers as well.

"Mama, are these birds here every day?"

"No, these are our spring birds,
I'm happy to say.
Some birds do stay
In our area all of the year,
While others fly south for the winter
And are not here.
The Nuthatch, Cardinal, Titmouse,
and Chickadee
Stay with us all year long as you will see."

The Red-winged Black Bird,
And Ruby-throated Hummingbird all,
Leave for warmer grounds
Early in fall.

While in winter the
Robin and Blue Jay
Sometimes will be seen
Often hiding deep in the woods,
Perhaps in a tree,
But...

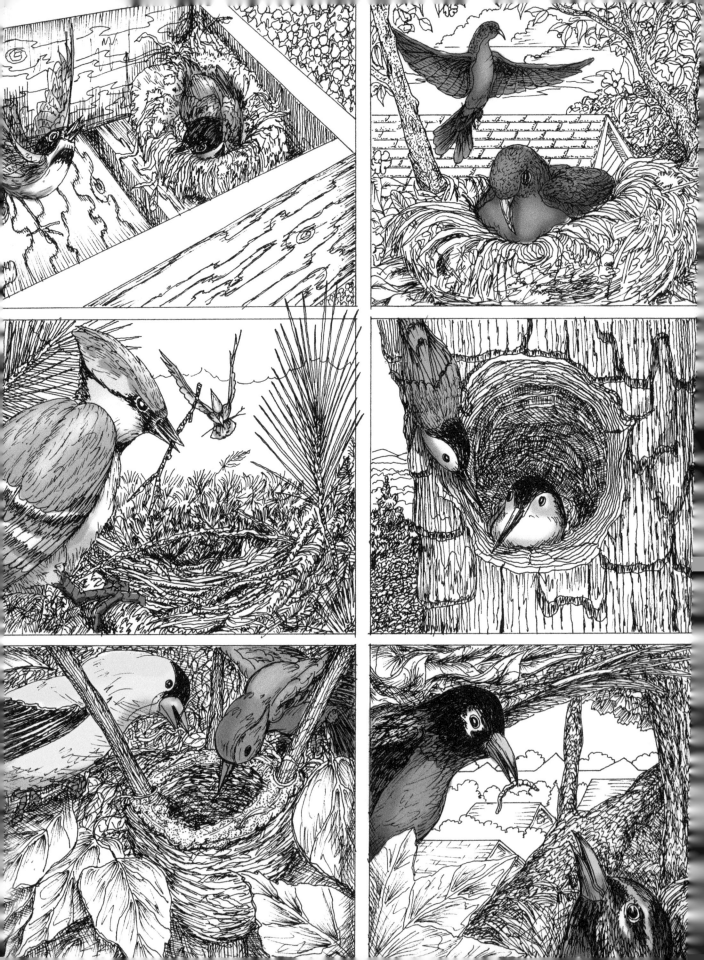

...All birds sing most
In the coolness of spring,
Setting up territories and
Looking for mates
as they sing.
And we are all lucky
To learn
To enjoy their song...

...And appreciate
The different birds
We see and hear
Each spring
And
All year long.